Gadgets and Gizmos

**Stories by Sally Odgers,
Michael Pryor and Rory Barnes**

Ginn is a registered trademark of Harcourt Education Ltd

Linacre House, Jordan Hill, Oxford, OX2 8DP
a division of Harcourt Education Ltd

Visit www.myprimary.co.uk to see a chart showing you all the Pocket Reads programme information you will need.

Station Starside One © Sally Odgers 1999
Room for Improvement © Michael Pryor 1999
Ghosting © Rory Barnes 2002

From the Spinouts project developed by Paul Collins and Meredith Costain.

This book is copyright and reproduction of the whole or part without the publisher's written permission is prohibited.

08 07
10 9 8 7 6 5 4 3 2

ISBN 0 602 24306 8 / 978 0 602 243 06 7

Station Starside One illustrated by Grant Gittus
Room for Improvement illustrated by Terry Denton
Ghosting illustrated by Louise Prout

Cover illustration by Marc McBride

Designed by Carolyn Gibson

Repro by Digital Imaging, Glasgow

Printed and bound in China through Phoenix Offset

CONTENTS

About Sally Odgers — 4

Station Starside One — 5

About Michael Pryor — 20

Room for Improvement — 21

About Rory Barnes — 35

Ghosting — 36

About Sally Odgers

Sally lives in Tasmania with her husband, their children, and several friends who happen to have paws and beaks. Sally loves fantasy and sci-fi.

About the story

"Why do we do that? Why do we believe this? It's tradition! Traditions fascinate me, so I wrote a story about one that was misunderstood and plain worn out."

Station Starside One

by Sally Odgers

Station Starside One was sparkling new. It sailed silently through its orbit, the home of thousands of people. And every person had been born on the great generation ship that made the one-way journey from Earth.

The Station had radio contact, and Earth Central sent a vid-link. At first, Stationers used this to keep in touch, but eventually the vid-link screen was abandoned in the disused loading bay.

Much later, Starsides Two and Three were launched. Space-skipper ships were invented, and used for commuting back and forth to Earth. Earth Central considered offering space-skippers to the people of SS1, but what was the point? They never made contact now. They never used the vid-link screen. Obviously, they wanted privacy.

Better to leave them alone …

Three centuries later, Pria's robot Hurryup fell down an ancient grav-shaft in SS1's forgotten sector. "Fall down, me!" he clanked. "Pria help Hurryup!"

"Bother!" said Pria. It was a long way down, but Hurryup was her best friend, a present from Grandfadda. She tested the grav-shaft by dropping a rusty bolt into it, then jumped in and drifted to the round grey room below.

"Hurt, me." Hurryup creaked his metal limbs.

"Rubbish," said Pria, hugging him. "Robo-pets are indestructible." The room was empty, with a round groove in the floor. Next to it was a panel in a swivelling frame. It was dull silver, covered with dust, with sliding switches and dials on top. The switches were stiff, but Pria shoved one over, making the panel swirl and ripple. She tried a dial. It hardly moved, but the frame lit up and red letters began to blink in its rim.

"MAL-FUNCT-ION-MAL-FUNCT-ION-MAL-FUNCT-ION."

Hurryup whirred and clanked excitedly. "Pria, signal make!"

The letters were changing to amber as Pria backed away. "VID-TECH-DE-SPATCH-ING-VID-TECH-DE-SPATCH-ING." Then they were green. "VID-TECH-AR-RIV-ING-VID-TECH-AR-RIV-ING." The grooved section of floor fell away and a weird round vehicle rose through the gap. Pria cowered against the wall as a figure got out of the vehicle, removed its helmet, turned and smiled at her. It was a stranger, a boy of about her age.

"I'm Jik," he said. "I'm your vid-link screen service technician."

"You – you *what*?" she stammered.

"I'm a service technician, and you know what? I qualified yesterday!" He grinned. "Never expected a call on my first day! What is this place?"

"SS1, of course."

"Spacestation Starside One!" Jik whistled. "I didn't know this place had a vid-link screen!"

"A what?"

"Vid-link screen." Jik pointed at the flashing panel. "When I picked up that malfunction beacon, I flipped the space-skipper to auto-track and hopped in. What's your name, and what's that you're holding?"

"I'm Pria, and this is Hurryup."

"No hurry me," clanked Hurryup.

Jik laughed, bending to examine the flashing screen. "Ugh – what a filthy antique! Gunk in the works, that's the trouble." Humming, he cleaned the panel, then adjusted the switches and dials. "That's better, but the focus is blurred. Which part of Earth shall we see, Pria?"

"Earth?" she said uncertainly. She had heard of Earth, of course, but she'd never expected to see it. "I don't know."

"I'll show you my home," decided Jik. He turned the dial. The screen brightened and a city swam into view, closer and closer, until Pria saw people in the streets. Some waved to her.

"That looks like our city," she said. "But who are the people?"

"Wait." Jik twiddled the dial. The city shifted sideways. Now the view showed one house, and a patch of green.

Pria cuddled Hurryup closely. "What are those big vegetables?"

"You mean trees?" said Jik.

"And that big stuff like water?"

"That's our pond." Jik stared at her. "Pria, haven't you used this screen before?"

"This is the forgotten sector. No one comes here. I'm only here because Hurryup fell down the grav-shaft."

Jik frowned as he adjusted the focus so Pria could see the pond.

"Oh!" said Pria longingly. "I've never seen anything like it!"

"Surely you get Earth-leave?" asked Jik. "Holidays on Earth?"

"How could we?"

"People from SS6 and SS7 do."

Pria couldn't imagine that. "They must be

much closer to Earth," she said.

Weird! Jik knew SS1 was the closest of the far-range stations. But that vid-link screen had been badly corroded, and there'd never been a service call from SS1 before. Had he made some terrible mistake in coming here?

"You called this place the forgotten sector. Does that mean you're not allowed to come here?"

"I don't think so." Pria shook back her hair. "Let's ask Grandfadda. He'll know."

Jik couldn't risk going with Pria. No one from Earth was allowed to enter a space station without invitation. "No. No, I don't think so. The screen's fine now," Jik said heartily. He adjusted the focus to the swirling standby pattern again. "Must go. Goodbye." He clamped on his helmet.

"Wait," said Pria. "What about asking Grandfadda?"

"Better not," said Jik. "Sorry, I shouldn't

have come." Hurriedly, he sealed himself into the space-skipper and left the docking bay.

That beacon must have been set off accidentally, he thought. He should never have answered it. It wasn't his fault, but he hoped his supervisor would understand.

Pria knelt by the blank vid-link screen. Earth! Wasn't it a lifetime away? No, because Jik lived there. She frowned as she clambered up the grav-shaft with Hurryup, and ran to Grandfadda's unit.

"Grandfadda, what do you know about Earth?"

Grandfadda looked surprised. "Not much, Pria. Why?"

"I met an Earthlie today." Pria explained about Jik and the vid-link screen.

Grandfadda's eyebrows shot up to his ginger hair. "In the forgotten sector, you say? Amazing! I'll see what I can find out."

Soon, Grandfadda found some answers. "According to the old records," said Grandfadda, "SS1 is the earliest spacestation in the Starside System."

"Of course," scoffed Pria. "That's why it's Station Starside *One*."

"It took the Earthlies a hundred years to bring SS1 into this orbit," said Grandfadda. "The first Stationers had travelled all their lives to get here. They knew there was no return to Earth."

"There is now," said Pria. "If Jik could visit us, we could visit Earth!"

"Obviously." Grandfadda sighed. "I suppose the idea of permanent exile was so strong that the first Stationers taught it to their children and it's been with us ever since! But Pria, you must face facts. The Earthlies don't want us to visit. If they did, they'd have invited us long ago."

"Ridiculous!" said Pria.

Grandfadda shrugged. "Traditions live

longer than people, Pria."

"So? Just because a tradition is old, doesn't mean it's good," she objected. "I'm going to visit Earth! Just you wait and see."

"How?" asked Grandfadda.

"I'll find a way."

Back on Earth, Jik confessed his mistake to his supervisor. "Pria triggered the beacon accidentally, I expect. She didn't understand."

"No harm done," said Marko kindly. "You responded to a malfunction call. That's what vid-techs do."

"Marko, why don't SS1 Stationers visit Earth?"

Marko shrugged. "I guess they like to keep themselves to themselves, Jik."

"Pria had never seen a tree or a pond!"

"Presumably she doesn't want to. The SS1 Stationers have ignored us for centuries. They don't care about us."

"I could have invited Pria for a visit," muttered Jik. "In fact, I think I will."

"You know the penalties for interfering, Jik!"

"I've managed to get there once."

"Genuine mistakes can be overlooked, but your job is to service vid-link screens, not to upset people."

Pria was still determined to visit Earth, but how? She hoped Jik might come back and advise her, but he didn't.

Grandfadda couldn't help, so Pria and Hurryup spent hours in the old docking bay, trying to work the vid-link screen. Sometimes Pria thought she saw glimpses of Earth, but she could never bring them into focus.

"Bother it, Hurryup! There must be some way to make it work!" she complained.

"MAL-FUNCT-ION-MAL-FUNCT-ION-MAL-FUNCT-ION," hummed Hurryup.

"Not any more. It's mended. I just can't work it!"

"Pria signal male!" said Hurryup brightly.

"Another malfunction signal? I suppose I *could*." Pria grinned. "Clever, clever Hurryup! I've been trying to make it work properly, but it really should work *im*properly!"

Pria tried all the switches and dials. They all moved easily, and nothing happened.

"Works gunk in," said Hurryup.

Pria thought for a moment. "Gunk in the works!" she whooped. "That's what we need!"

Pria swept up a pile of dust and rust and grit. She damped it down with oil from Hurryup's reserves then scrubbed it into the vid-link screen. Then she left it to set.

Two days later, she brought Grandfadda to see the screen. And this time, when she tried the dials, something happened!

"MAL-FUNCT-ION-MAL-FUNCT-ION-MAL-FUNCT-ION," flashed the red letters.

Hurryup whirred and clacked excitedly as the words blinked amber, and finally, green. "Pria, signal make!"

"VID-TECH-DE-SPATCH-ING-VID-TECH-DE-SPATCH-ING. VID-TECH-AR-RIV-ING-VID-TECH-AR-RIV-ING."

Pria danced with glee as the floor dropped and the space-skipper rose into view.

The vid-tech got out and unclamped his helmet. "I know you're not interested in Earth ..." he began warily.

"Rubbish!" said Pria. "Whoever told you that?"

"Marko says it's an old tradition," said Jik.

"A bad old tradition." Pria beamed at him. "This is Grandfadda, Jik, and of course you know Hurryup. And guess what! We four are about to start a new tradition!"

About Michael Pryor

Michael Pryor has worked in a scrap metal yard and as a truck driver, a tap salesman, an Internet consultant, a software developer and a teacher. He has published over 40 short stories and eight novels.

About the story

"I've always liked writing about characters who are quick on their feet. But then I started wondering about someone like that whose mouth tended to run away with them, and the trouble that could get them into …"

Michael Pryor

Room for Improvement

by Michael Pryor

Sarah sighed as she skated down the hill towards home. Her school bag was clumsy on her back and she thought she could hear the pieces of her calculator rattling around inside.

"Mum'll kill me," she muttered, and coasted around the corner. She neatly avoided the lamp post and powered up the footpath. "But it wasn't my fault."

The first part wasn't true, the second part was. The broken calculator wasn't her fault. It was Mandy Grundig's fault.

Lots of things were Mandy Grundig's fault; all the kids knew that. Squashed bananas in your schoolbag, broken rulers, missing pencils, that sort of thing was The Grunter's fault. And everything done with that mean smile that said: "You think that's bad? Just you wait."

And of course, The Grunter was huge. She loved lifting weights. She also liked dropping them on people.

The trouble was, The Grunter was plain mean. Sarah had tried being kind, tried ignoring her, tried everything. But still she suffered from The Grunter, like everyone else.

The calculator was the latest catastrophe, and all because Sarah had been daydreaming during Maths. "What are you looking at?" Mandy had hissed, and Sarah realised that she'd been looking in The Grunter's direction. And before Sarah could stop them, the words popped out of her mouth. "I think it's a giant slug, but I'm not sure."

As soon as she said it, Sarah knew she was doomed. But she never could stop her mouth. Sometimes it just had a life of its own. She put her head in her hands.

When the class finished, The Grunter stomped past Sarah's desk and knocked her calculator onto the floor.

Then she crushed it with her foot.

"Gee, sorry," The Grunter said greasily, then waddled off.

The memory made Sarah's stomach flip over, and she stopped for a moment outside the shops.

She saw that a new shop had opened, in between the old picture framer's and the abandoned pet shop. "FIXIT" it said in large letters, and underneath in smaller letters: "We Repair Anything!"

Sarah didn't think. She rolled right in.

Inside the small shop Sarah saw rows of shelves. On them were toasters, tennis racquets, fish tanks, watches, radios, shoes, bird cages and sewing machines. And all of them had parts missing, or were broken.

Behind the counter was a tall, thin woman, with hair the colour of a cloudy sky. "I'm Ms Fixit. What can I do for you?" she said, looking at Sarah over her glasses.

"Can you do calculators?" Sarah asked.

"The sign outside says 'Anything'," the woman said. "Let me see it."

Sarah handed over the mangled calculator, and the woman peered at it closely. "Five minutes," she announced, and disappeared through a curtained door.

She was back in two. "One pound, please."

"Will it work?" Sarah asked doubtfully.

"Better than ever," the woman said. Then she smiled. "Or your money back."

It was when Sarah was doing her homework that she noticed there was something strange going on with the calculator.

She could talk to it.

Sarah found this out because she always read Maths problems out aloud. And after she read out the first one, the numbers appeared on the calculator's tiny screen.

Sarah's eyes opened wide, and after she experimented a little, she believed it. She suddenly had a voice-activated calculator!

All the next day at school, Sarah thought about her calculator. Ms Fixit had certainly repaired it. In fact, it was better than ever.

Even The Grunter's efforts didn't distract Sarah. "Watchit, pimple," Mandy growled in the corridor, and elbowed Sarah in the back.

"I don't have to watch it, I can smell it," Sarah's mouth said, and The Grunter's face turned purple.

Sarah was saved by the headteacher, who happened to walk past, and Sarah scampered out of the door before The Grunter could mangle her.

Sarah scooted home as fast as her blades would take her. In the back of her wardrobe she found her old clock radio, the one that had stopped working when she'd accidentally dropped it in the fish tank.

"Not a problem," Ms Fixit declared when Sarah took it in the next day. "Soon it'll be better than ever."

"I'm looking forward to this," Sarah said when the spindly woman trotted back, and accepted the pound coin Sarah gave her.

Sarah had never been able to find an alarm that worked for her. She could stay asleep with a steam roller crushing a dozen pianos next to her. So that night she set the alarm eagerly.

And woke up to an earthquake.

The bed was shaking, her teeth were rattling, and she felt like she was inside a tumble drier.

With a thump she fell out of bed. "Good," a voice said. "It's about time."

Even though she was sitting on the cold floor with only her pyjamas on, Sarah chuckled. The voice had come from her improved clock radio. When she examined it, she found a small dial set into the base. She was sure it hadn't been there before. The dial had settings marked 'Earthquake', 'Thunderstorm', 'Hail' and 'Lightning'.

She shuddered and gently put down the machine. There was no way she wanted to be crisped by a lightning bolt in bed!

As she skated to school, Sarah thought hard. The improvements to her calculator and clock radio were amazing. "Magical," she said.

That was when she sped around a blind corner and ran into The Grunter.

As Sarah bounced off her and sailed through the air, she found herself thinking, "I've got a serious problem."

She landed painfully on her shoulder, then slid along the footpath on her back. Her schoolbag felt like it had a few bales of barbed wire in it.

When she opened her eyes, she saw The Grunter standing over her. She was so big she blotted out the sun.

"You!" The Grunter snarled, looking as if her muscles were about to explode. "You again!"

Sarah scrambled to her feet, barely avoiding The Grunter's massive arms.

"Come back here!" The Grunter roared as Sarah ducked. "Your time is up!"

"Really?" said Sarah. "What number is the big hand on?"

"You're history!"

"At least it's better than being pastry. Has anyone ever told you that you have a face like a meat pie? With sauce?"

Sarah glided backwards as The Grunter tottered after her. She could hardly believe what her own mouth was saying. Did I really call The

Grunter a pie face? she thought with dismay. I should wear a gag.

Then Sarah noticed that The Grunter was wearing blade skates. They looked like baby boots on an elephant, because her feet were the only tiny thing about her. Sarah knew that The Grunter's feet were the same size as hers, because The Grunter had borrowed Sarah's trainers one day in PE. Without asking, of course.

But Sarah found she could easily stay out of The Grunter's reach. Her enemy was just a clumsy beginner. "I'd love to stop and chat," Sarah grinned, "but I've got people I can do that with."

The screech that followed Sarah down the street was enough to crack glass. I've done it again, Sarah thought. Why can't I keep my big mouth shut?

When school finished, Sarah grabbed her blades. A note fluttered out as they fell to pieces. "Let's see how well you can skate with these, Motor Mouth."

Sarah didn't have to see a signature to know it was the work of The Grunter. She frowned, but her face soon cleared. "Another job for Ms Fixit," she said aloud, and sprinted down the road with her broken blades.

"Ah, Sarah," said the repairer. "I knew you'd be back."

"Here," Sarah panted. "My blades. Broken."

Ms Fixit waved her hand. "I know that, I know that. But I fix more important things than machines, you know."

"You do?" Sarah asked.

"Problems, for example. I fix problems."

Sarah stared. "How?" she asked.

Ms Fixit raised an eyebrow. "Now, that's the thing. You don't know how until it's fixed. Do you have any problems, Sarah?"

Sarah thought about a problem she had. A problem the size of a mountain. And twice as mean.

"Yes," she said firmly. "But I just want my blades fixed, thanks. I can handle my problems myself."

"Now, that's what I like to hear. As soon as you say that, your problem's half solved." She chuckled again. "Of course, a little help never hurts." And whistling, she disappeared into her back room.

When Ms Fixit came back, she had two small robots in her hands. At least, they looked like robots. After a moment's staring, Sarah recognised them as her blades.

They were covered with bright chrome, and had sprockets and flanges sticking out at all angles.

"Now they're better than ever. One pound, please."

In a daze, Sarah paid and stumbled out of the shop. She stood blinking in the sunlight, holding her improved blades as if they might blast off at any minute.

"Thanks. I'll just take those." The voice was snarly, mean, and it belonged to The Grunter.

"Hey!" Sarah cried. "They're mine!"

"Well, I'll just borrow them for a while. Say five or six years," The Grunter smirked.

Sarah watched helplessly as The Grunter strapped the blades on her muscly legs. "I don't think you should do that," she began.

"Too late!" cried The Grunter, and stood up, arms waving to keep her balance.

The burst of light from the back of the skates took Sarah by surprise. An ear-splitting scream followed.

Then, with smoke pouring from the skates, The Grunter started rolling faster and faster. Up the hill.

Her pace grew rapidly until she was a blur of speed. When she reached the top of the hill, she took off.

Sarah watched as The Grunter's smoke trail stretched across the sky. Soon, she'd lost sight of the tiny dot her enemy had become.

"Problem solved," Sarah said, and heard a small, soft popping noise from behind her. When she turned, the magical repair shop had gone.

Sarah shrugged, and looked at the sky again. "Yes, a definite improvement."

About Rory Barnes

Rory Barnes was born in London, but has lived most of his life in Australia. He used to work in schools and universities, but now writes full-time.

About the story

"I've always liked stories in which the underdog suddenly turns into a rebel. Watching my son's broken-down, second-hand telly one day, I thought: wouldn't it be wonderful if the ghost images on the screen suddenly started doing things differently from the 'real' images? So I wrote a story in which this happened."

Ghosting

by Rory Barnes

There's a second-hand shop on the way home from school. It's run by an old guy with an eye-shade. I don't know his name. Sometimes I buy used CDs from him. Sometimes I just check out the stuff in the window.

One day there was a wicked television sitting bang in the middle of the electric drills and the dodgy-looking cameras. The telly only had a small screen, but the cabinet was made of this dark, polished timber and the knobs were really retro. They could have been the controls of a hot air balloon. The price tag said it all: £5. Five quid! I even had that amount in my wallet. Well, almost.

I ducked into the shop and put a proposition to the eye-shade guy. "Lend me a trolley and I'll take that old telly off you for £4.70," I said.

"Done," said the old guy, and took all my money. "I hope you like ghosts," he said as I was wheeling my new possession out of the door.

"Ghosts?" I said.

"Yeah," he said. "Those old sets are a bit prone to ghosting."

"I can cope," I said.

I pushed the telly home. I'll say this – it was a monster. Nothing slimline about my new friend. And it was heavy. But I got it into my bedroom and plugged it in.

It took a bit of time to warm up. But slowly a picture emerged. They were showing an old black and white movie – funny old cars and cops in old-fashioned uniforms. I switched channels. Another ancient black and white film. I tried again, but I could only get two channels.

I watched the cop show for a bit. The film ended and the announcer came on. He was a funny young guy with too much hair and a paisley tie. And he was still in black and white. He started to read the news. There was a shot of a rocket on a launch pad. The newsreader's voice said that the countdown at Cape Canaveral was proceeding and Apollo would be taking off for the moon in just under two hours. The astronauts were in good shape.

The moon! No astronauts had been to the moon for ages. What was this guy on about?

My sister came into the room and laughed her head off. "What's that?" she said.

"It's my new telly," I said.

"New!" she said. "It looks like something Noah had on the ark. The animals used to watch that thing while they were waiting for the floodwaters to go down."

"Oh, very funny," I said.

"It's so old," she said, "it only shows old programmes. Look at that! They're not even using a proper space shuttle."

"It's a history programme," I said. "It's showing how people used to live in the old days."

"I'll bet it's not on the real telly," my sister said, and left the room. I could hear her in the living room, surfing the channels. "No," she yelled after half a minute, "that old rubbish is only on your set."

This was weird. Maybe I'd bought some sort of primitive video machine. I checked all the controls. It wasn't a video. It was a television set. It was a television set that was showing programmes that were broadcast years and years ago.

"Pity it doesn't show the future," my sister said, coming back into the room. "That way we could win the lottery."

"Maybe it does show the future," I said.

"Oh, yeah," she said.

"I only said *maybe*."

"Give me a shout when you get the news for the year 2020," my sister said and went back to the living room.

I thought I'd better inspect the telly properly. I looked at the retro knobs. There wasn't anything very odd about them. They did the normal things: contrast, brightness, volume, channels (all two of them). I looked at the back of the machine. No more switches.

Just a notice in faded writing that said, "No human repairs possible – do not open."

Talk about weird. If humans can't repair televisions, who can? And I don't like being told not to open things. I reckoned it was about time I had a look inside. I went out to the garden shed and got a screwdriver. As I was passing though the living room my sister said, "Got the 2020 news yet?"

"Nah," I said. "I'm only up to 2019."

"Boring," my sister said, and went on watching a full colour video-clip on the family's telly.

Back in my bedroom, I switched my telly off at the wall socket and unplugged it for good measure. Then I unscrewed the back. Talk about old-fashioned! This baby still had valves: great big glass tubes with wires and bits of funny silver cardboard. A couple of them were still glowing. I took a closer look. I soon found a couple more switches, half hidden amongst all the old wires and valves.

Both switches had two positions. One switch was labelled *Time* and was pointing to PAST. The other switch was labelled *Ghosts* and was pointing to OFF.

Quick as a flash I turned the *Time* switch so that it pointed to FUT (I reckoned that was short for FUTURE). I looked at the other switch but didn't touch it. Why would anyone actually *want* to get a ghost effect on their screen? They'd have to be mad.

I was about to screw the back panel into place, when I changed my mind. That switch had to be there for a purpose. It would be interesting to see what happened. I turned the *Ghosts* switch to ON.

I replaced the back panel and turned the telly on. Nothing happened. I didn't expect it to. I sat there on the floor in front of the set waiting for the valves to warm up again.

Suddenly, bingo! There was a full-colour picture on the screen. What a picture! Crystal clear and in three dimensions. I was looking at a park scene so brilliant I could have been looking out of a window, not at a screen. This just had to be the future.

I was about to yell out to my sister, when I noticed something odd. There was a guy walking along a path and he was being followed very closely by ... well, he was being followed by a ghost. It was just like the ordinary double images you sometimes get on television. There was a faint outline of the guy off to one side. But the funny thing was that only the guy had this double-image ghost. The trees and fountains in the park were all as clear and sharp as a picture can be.

I just sat there watching. The camera moved. Now there were more people in the park. They all had ghosts. One old lady was walking a dog on a lead. The dog had a ghost too.

A guy on a really cool skateboard went gliding down a path, followed by his ghost. The guy on the skateboard overtook the old lady with the dog. The real dog took no notice of the skateboard guy. But the ghost dog did.

The ghost dog broke free from the real dog and bit the ghost skateboarder on the leg. The ghost skateboarder fell off his board and started kicking the ghost dog. They were snarling and kicking. But the real humans and the real dog just kept on going – without their ghosts.

I couldn't believe what I was seeing. Then suddenly the blurry, biting, kicking ghosts broke up the fight and hurried to catch up with their owners. They fell into line. Once again they were doing exactly what the real skateboarder and the real dog were doing.

I changed channels. There was some sort of science programme in brilliant 3D colour. The presenter was standing in a street that looked a bit like ours. She had a ghost. The ghost was just to one side of her, mouthing the same words the presenter was saying.

"The small meteorite crashed to Earth in this suburban street ten years ago today," the presenter said. "It smashed a hole in the roof of a house and destroyed a bedroom. Luckily, no one was at home."

Suddenly the presenter's ghost stopped mouthing the words. The ghost looked horrified. The ghost looked panicked. The ghost looked straight at me.

Suddenly the ghost was mouthing a whole lot of different words. But I couldn't understand her. There was a shot of the house. It was our house.

Then the presenter was back on the screen. And the ghost presenter was going mad, yelling soundlessly at me. I looked at her mouth, trying to lip-read.

Then I got it. I understood what she was saying: "Get out of your house, get out, now!"

I ran into the living room. I grabbed my sister's wrist and started hauling.

"Let go!" she yelled.

But I didn't. I hauled her out into the street. I ran, pulling my sister along. My sister ran

beside me, yelling at me to let go, hitting at me with her free hand.

We'd got about a hundred metres when there was a violent bang behind us. The shock wave knocked us flying. We sat in the road and looked back. There was a jagged hole in the

roof of our house. All the windows had been blown out. There was dust everywhere.

"Meteorite," I gasped.

"How did you know?" my sister demanded.

"It was on my telly," I said.

"*Before* it happened?"

"Yeah," I gasped. "I switched the telly to FUT."

"PHUT!" yelled my sister. "You moron. Don't you know what PHUT means? You blew that telly up. You've half-wrecked our house!"